CW01431822

Camping Hacks:
The Top 20+ Hacks For Camping, Backpacking and Other Outdoor Adventures

Table of Contents

* * * * * * * * * * * * * * * * * * *

Introduction: What Every Good Camper Should Know

You can rest assured that even under the best of conditions, your camping excursion could have a few surprises for you. This is simply the state of nature, and we are all living in a state of controlled chaos. You can never completely mitigate the unforeseen, but the better you know how to control it, the better off you will be. That's exactly where this book comes in; the contents of this book will serve as your guide.

The 20 hacks presented here are just as pragmatic as they are practical, and you never have to worry as long as you keep them close to your heart. Even if right now you feel like you aren't the best hiker, you are lousy at pitching a tent, and you couldn't build a campfire to save your life, the 20 hacks presented in this book will provide you with the blueprints you need to get through some of the most challenging situations you may face on the camp grounds.

Many of us, as we live in our increasingly urbanized societies find ourselves increasingly out of sync with nature. A fact that becomes painfully evident when you decide to go camping for the first time, or even the first time in a long time, as you realize just how environmentally tone deaf you are. That why the next few chapters are so important, they will help to bring you back in tune with the great outdoors; bringing you back to what every good camper should know.

Chapter 1: Know How to Navigate your Campsite

Knowing your way around the campgrounds is a must. I've learned the hard way how easy it is to get disoriented in unknown terrain, s take it from me, its not hard to get turned around. In order to avoid the headache of losing your way, you need to keep up your concentration and use all the right tools at your disposal to stay on track. And even if you do happen to become disoriented, you need to know how to pull yourself out of your disorientation. This chapter shows you how you can effectively find your way no matter where you end up!

Use Topographical Maps

The highway map in your glove box may be helpful during a road trip but when you are hiking out in the wilderness its no better than walking around with a phone book. All of those city and highway markings mean nothing when you are trying to navigate through hills, streams, and trees. This is why knowing how to use a topographical map is so important.

When you know how to read the contour lines on a topographical map you can pinpoint exactly where you are at any given time. These maps use special colors and lines to illustrate where hills and dips in the land are, as well as wooded areas. Specially shaded lines of brown are indicative of elevation, and can demonstrate great changes in terrain. No matter where you are, it's a great boon to have one of these maps on hand. So be sure to pack this hack in your backpacking backpack! (Now try saying that ten times fast!)

Bring Binoculars

The usefulness of binoculars shouldn't be discounted. If you ever have trouble figuring out where you are, you can use a pair of binoculars to scope out the territory, seeing further than you normally can. If you lose track of the campsite for example, just one look with a good set of binoculars and you could probably catch sight of it once again.

Binoculars work by focusing as much sunlight as possible through the binocular lens, and into your line of vision. They are a great asset to have. Our natural vision can only go so far, but with this one handy hack we can extend our natural abilities immensely.

Know How to Use Your Compass

Probably the most important tool of navigation you could ever use, the compass is your assurance that you will at all times have a reliable sense of direction. This tool points you to the West, East, South, and the North without a problem. But to say that the standard compass points directly to the north would actually be a bit of a misnomer. Because what it is that the standard magnetized compass is actually pointing to is the "Magnetic North" of the planet's North Pole.

And Magnetic North is slightly off center from the actual North Pole of the planet. If you wanted to be more precise about it, you would have to take into account this magnetic declination, but these are just minor details, and you usually don't have to be so technical. And when you are trekking into the wilderness in Northern Minnesota, you could most likely get by just fine with the "general" direction of north that the standard compass provides.

These kinds of compasses can be found at just about any good department or hardware store, but if you don't want to buy one, you could just as easily make one yourself. In order to do so, just get out a good needle (as in needle and thread) and rub it against a piece of cloth until it has become magnetized. Now just put this bad boy in water and; voila! Instant compass! These sorts of home-made compasses can be made anywhere, and used in any environment, so make sure to make this hack a part of your camping regimen.

Chapter 2: Cooking and Keeping Warm with Your Campfire

Camping is no fun if you can't keep warm and you can't even cook your food. Many like to start up campfires with prefabricate materials, and that's fine, but just in case you find yourself in a pinch, you really need to know how to make your campfires from scratch. This chapter will focus on teaching you how to do just that.

Fire Drills

No I'm not speaking of all those times in elementary school that you filed out in the cold to rehearse what you would do if your school was ablaze, I'm speaking of the actual fire drill instrument that can help you spark a campfire. The fire drill I speak of his basically a long skinny stick that you roll between your hands over another piece of wood (drilling the stick into wood) until you can successfully spark a fire.

These fire drills can be made from brush in the natural environment or they can be purchased from DIY stores. Once you catch a spark with one of these guys you can then groom it into a full blown campfire in no time. Just repeat this process whenever you need to start a campfire. It's easy, it doesn't take much time to use, and it doesn't deplete any extra resources in order to use it (the woods are usually full of sticks). If you learn this simple hack, you will never go cold again.

The Power of Flint

In many ways, even better than a fire drill, if you have a good piece of flint rock you can achieve much the same result, with much less work. All you have to do is strike this rock against a hard surface and it will immediately shoot out sparks that can be captured by your kindle (not your tablet folks, I'm talking about firewood) and bring your campfire to life.

Using flint is especially useful if it is particularly windy where you are, since wind can greatly hamper other fire starting methods. Flint still works in even the windiest of conditions. So make sure you have a flint rock or two in your supply. You can just shove this rock in your pocket and save it for when you need it. It's a simple hack that can save you a lot of trouble in the long run.

Creating a Wilderness Fireplace

In order to make your campsite more of a permanent locale you should create a solid wilderness fireplace that can be used multiple times. The easiest way to establish this is to use a circle of stones as the base for your fireplace. Simply gather up a bunch of medium sized stones and place them in a circle.

Inside of your stone boundary then place your kindling that you will use to start your fire. These stones not only mark your campsite they also serve to make sure your campfire doesn't get out of control, keeping it safely contained within the circular framework of your wilderness fireplace. This peace of mind will allow you to go to sleep in the warmth of your fire without any fear of the flames escaping your designated area for the campfire.

The fireplace is also a great place to cook your food. It provides proper structure, and even works to focus the flames more intensely on what you are cooking. It's particularly useful when attempting to sear meat. Just put a slab of meat on a stick and let it roast over the open fire. I love cooking outdoors with a homemade wilderness fireplace. No other camping hack has ever made a rabbit taste as good!

Using A Power Pot

I wanted to close this chapter with a bit of an alternative to the traditional campground equipment. Let me introduce to you the "power-pot" this little guy can cook your food no matter where you are and while it cooks you can even plug your phone into it! Yes, that's right! The power pot has a USB port and the built in capability to convert the energy from a boiling pot, into direct energy to your phone. You can cook up a pot of stew and play angry birds all at the same time! This hack really is a wonderful idea!

Chapter 3: Campground Communication

Even at a remote campground you should still have at least some handle on communication. In case you get into some kind of emergency you need to be able to contact the outside world. This chapter presents some of the ways you can maintain and establish and maintain an outside communication link while you camp. So here it is folks, the very best in campground communication!

Using Smoke Signals

If you have nothing else, smoke signals can work out as a great communication tool. This means of communication has a large range, and can be used to signal help from many miles away. So if you get lost in the woods, feel free to smoke out some assistance from the skies! And besides SOS signals, if you know what to do, you can send out entire coded messages, just with a few puffs of smoke. Look out NASA! This smoky communiqué is so clear, even the space aliens might try to decode these signals!

Producing Emergency Flares

Working on and expanding the premise of the smoke signal, the emergency flare can be seen from hundreds of miles and will most certainly get the word out when you need assistance. The blinding luminosity of the flare can be seen during night or day. So make sure you put at least one in you backpack before you set off for your adventure in the wilderness. Just one of these flares could make the difference between life and death. This is a hack you have got to pack!

Employing a Satellite Phone

The satellite phone is admittedly, a rather luxurious communication tool to bring along to a camping trip, but if you can afford one, it could prove invaluable. Because as long as that satellite is up in space sending a constant feed to your phone, you could quite literally be *anywhere* on the planet and still give your best buds a call! Just think about it! There is no one who wouldn't be within your reach. But with great power comes great responsibility! (Or at least that's what Spiderman told me!)

So if you are going to be late coming back from the end of a two week vacation in the Amazon Jungle, you still have to have the wherewithal to call you boss back home! Just call that mean old supervisor right up on your Sat and tell him, "Sorry Boss, but I can't make it to work today because I'm still spear fishing piranhas out of the Amazon River!" (Or then again, maybe don't do that!) At any rate, the satellite phone is an ingenious communication tool!

Working a Hand Cranked Radio

By using nothing more than your hand you can crank this radio to life! Just the kinetic energy that you create with the motion of your hand is enough to charge up this radio. With a communication asset like this, you can be completely out of electricity and yet still have a fully functioning radio at your disposal.

For long duration hikes, when you would like to have a weather report long after your cell phone and other battery based electronics have gone dead, you will be glad to be able to crank this radio to life. And as an added bonus, after many hours of utilizing this hack you will have a killer set of biceps to boot!

Chapter 4: Campground Items for Common Health

Simply enough, camping is not fun if you don't feel good. Before you go camping, health should be of primary focus. You never know what could happen, so just in case you break an arm, sprain your ankle or have an allergic reaction at the campgrounds, you need to have a game plan as to what you might do to in the face of such contingencies. This chapter shows you how.

First Aid Kit

A good First Aid Kit is an invaluable hack, and should be one of the first thing you pack on any back packing adventure. The first aid kit should be your go to source for any health problem you face. Here you should store common (but extremely useful) health items such as Tylenol, cold packs, hydrogen peroxide, adhesive tape, scissors, tweezers, and simple needles and thread.

The Tylenol is great to bring down any inflammation, hydrogen peroxide is an excellent disinfectant, cold packs are good for aches and pains such as a strained ankle, and your adhesive tape is necessary to bandage any wounds. But most importantly having a good set of needles and thread could save your life in case you need to sow stitches for any unforeseen injury. This hack is essential, and doesn't take up much space, so make sure you don't leave home without a good First Aid Kit on hand.

Aloe Vera

Aloe Vera, whether cut straight from a plant or bottled up as gel, could be a lifesaving hack when you really need it! If you have ever suffered from a burn and had this soothing substance applied to your skin, you know the difference that it can make. As well as making burns and cuts feel better, Aloe Vera works to disinfect them and speeds up the healing process. And just a little dab will do you; it doesn't take much to make a difference. So either buy a bottle of this wonder gel at your local pharmacy or cut a few Aloe Vera leaves for yourself ahead of time. This is a hack you shouldn't do without!

Ginger

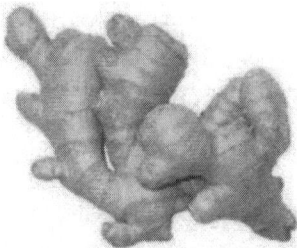

Ginger is a powerful remedy when it comes to curing simple aches and pains such as sprained ankles and pulled back muscles. Having a bit of this herb with you is a good hack for your health. This herb can also be boiled into healthy teas right over your campfire that can help alleviate many health problems you may encounter during your trek into the wilderness. It has been found to reduce nausea and is helpful with other digestive issues. This can be of great benefit when you are far away from drug stores and over the counter Pepto-Bismol! Make sure to pack this hack!

Garlic

Garlic is kind of a wonder herb and has many uses. Eating it—among other things —can actually work to detoxify your body. It is the heavy sulfur compounds present in garlic. Garlic has even been shown to greatly reduce lead, and could hypothetically be used as a treatment for lead poisoning. In fact, a recent study conducted with employees at a power plant, showed that those who regularly consumed garlic had a 20% lower level of lead in their blood than those who did not!

Garlic is good for our blood in other ways as well, since it has an uncanny ability of lowering blood pressure. Garlic is also known to greatly improve the immune system. Studies have shown regular consumption of garlic to reduce colds as much as 75% when compared to non-garlic consumers.

But heck, my own grandfather could have told you that! The old man used to string up a bunch of garlic into a necklace and wear it around his neck as a poultice. You didn't smell very good wearing it, and it was probably potent enough to ward off vampires, but it sure took care of that runny nose! Garlic is a natural cold and flu buster, so be sure to keep this healthy hack around for whatever ails you!

Chapter 5: Have A readily Made Water and Food Supply

Humans consume both food and water on a regular basis, and unless you are some sort of space alien reading this wilderness guide, I'm sure you are already aware of that little fact! These facts do not change when you go to the campgrounds or some other wilderness environment, if anything, they are exacerbated. After long hikes and prolonged exposure to the elements you may find yourself literally dying of thirst.

And no matter how much you might pack with you, supplies eventually run out, so this chapter will teach you the kind of hacks you need to know so that you can find your own food and water directly from the environment, so no matter where you are, you never have to do without again. Use the hacks presented in this chapter so you will always have a readily made *and reliable* water and food supply on hand.

Extract Water From Plants

This is a rather ingenious hack when it comes to getting some water. On the surface it seems simple enough, plants have water, and therefore you can easily extract water from them! But many have died in the wilderness from dehydration without even giving this little hack a second thought. So take note, now have how you can milk the plants in your environment of their H2O and you just might save your life tomorrow!

It's not hard at all; you just have to take a piece of absorbent cloth and use it to soak moisture off of any plant-life you encounter. You can then squeeze the moisture out into a cup, or if the situation is really dire, just squeeze it right into your mouth. It isn't the most sophisticated way to quench your thirst but it does the trick when it comes to staving off dehydration. I've known people that were forced to use their own socks as an H2O sponge in order to survive.

It's obviously not the most glamorous thing to do, but if worse comes to worse, it will keep you alive. And if you want to get more technical with this hack you can up the ante a bit, by attaching what is known as a "transpiration bag" to the plant. Basically this means taking a plastic bag and attaching it to a piece of foliage and leaving it overnight to drain as much liquid as you can from the plant. This happens through the natural process of evaporation, allowing the bag to collect any liquid that arises from the plant material.

Use Tarp to Collect Rainwater

One of the best ways to capture rain when you are out in the middle of the wilderness somewhere is to just spread out a nice big piece of tarp and let it collect the rain as it naturally falls down from the sky. To achieve this hack just evenly spread out your tarp and then nail each corner of it to a stake stuck in the ground. This will hold the tarp in place and allow it to collect the rain that pours down from above.

Just make sure that your tarp is a few inches above ground-level and you are in business. Before you know it, rain will begin collecting on your tarp, pooling right to the center of the material. To collect this newfound water source, just put a large container at the mouth of the tarp and let the water slide right down inside of it. It's a hack you can't live without! This is a must have hack!

Use Solar Sills

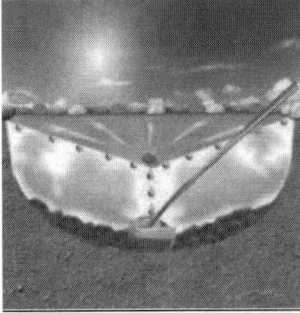

Another hack that can help you get some water in the wilderness is the Solar Sill. It's another simple, yet ingenious idea. In order to utilize this hack you need to dig a hole in the ground and then place a piece of plastic (trash bags work just fine) over the hole and then put rocks on the edges of the hole to hold the plastic in place. This is the basic structure of your solar sill.

You can then place a bunch of chopped up foliage into the center and it again, due to the process of evaporation, when solar radiation from the sun hits the sill, the liquid from these plants will collect on the tarp. This process is basically a proactive combination of the first two hacks since you are using both a large collection material similar to the tarp and you are forcibly extracting water from plants. This method just creates a lot more water, a lot faster.

Employ Fishing Spears

This hack is an easy way to get your fill of fish. Without even a fishing pole to rely on, if you can just sharpen up a stick, and quickly stab through a fresh stream you are bound to eventually strike some fishy gold. To unlock this hack, simply requisition a stick about 4 feet long, and sharpen it to a sharp point. Its just like sharpening a pencil.

Next, locate a fresh body of water in the middle of the day when the fish are most likely swimming in force and launch your spear into the waters. As long as you are precise with your lunges, and don't make too many waves, the fish don't even seem too disturbed by it. And with a little effort and a lot of luck, this hack will bring dinner back to the camp every single time you employ it!

Use Animal Traps

I know that it may seem a little bit cruel to set traps for animals, but when you are in a situation that calls for sheer survival, you may not have a choice. The woodlands have an abundance of wildlife, whether flying through the air, scurrying through the fields or climbing up trees. These small mammals have enough nutrition to keep you strong for several days, if you have no other food resource available you better put some of your ideological qualms aside and utilize this hack.

One of the easiest traps to employ is the simple, "Large Rock /Stick Trap". Much as the name implies, in order to create this trap, find a large rock and then prop it up with a stick. That's pretty much it. You could put some kind of food down under the rock as bait, but you usually don't even need to do that. Really all you have to do is prop a big rock up in an area heavily traveled by small animals and sooner rather than later some little critters will come nosing around and knock the rock right on top of his unfortunate head.

Well, as already discussed, in a true wilderness survival situation, beggars (and even campers) can't always be choosers. And having a few simple animal traps set out head of time can greatly ensure that you survive your backpacking, outdoor adventures, safe and secure. So don't underestimate the usefulness of this animal trap hack!

Learn to Forage

If you really can't hack it when it comes to eating wild meat, then there is another option for you; you can forage. Because in almost any wide open wilderness, there is bound to be plenty of food simply growing up out of the ground and hanging from trees. You just have to know where to find it. Berries and walnuts typically abound in the forest, and mushrooms and dandelions can be found just about everywhere else. Most of the wild plants you see growing in the wilderness are completely safe to consume.

But having that said, the most important thing in this hack is to know when and when *not to eat* a potential wild food source. Because although they are rare; there are a few things that could be deadly if eaten. In order to safeguard yourself form this, you will need to conduct routine taste tests in order to make sure the food is safe. This means that if you find yourself at all unsure about something that you have foraged, you should cut a small piece of it off.

Take this piece and rub it in the palm of your hand, if you do not have an immediate adverse reaction, put it in your mouth. Don't swallow the morsel, just let it sit on your tongue for about 30 seconds, if you can hold the food on your tongue for 30 seconds without a bad taste, swelling or any other allergic reaction go ahead and swallow it.

Now wait a few more minutes to make sure you don't feel nauseous. If your stomach holds up after five minutes or so, try to eat a larger piece of what you have foraged. Again, wait a few minutes to see how your stomach reacts; if you have passed through all of these sensory tests so far completely unscathed, then you can rest assured that this foraged food is safe to eat. Keep all of these hacks in mind as you embark on your camping trip.

Conclusion: You can Hack it!

The adventures we take outdoors are a time for us to relax and reflect in the comfort of nature. It shouldn't be a time of peril and hazard. And yet unfortunately, campground tragedies and backpacking and hiking disasters seem to be on the increase. There seems to be an increasing number of people taking the up the invitation of the great outdoors, but yet they are woefully unprepared once they get there.

It doesn't have to be that way however. As this book has demonstrated there is a solution to just about anything you could encounter, if you just no where to look. So even if you get lost in the woods, you run out of food and water, and you break your leg (hopefully not) you will nevertheless be prepared! You will know what to do in an emergency.

If you have read this book and taken the life lessons presented here to heart, there is no reason why you won't be able to face any obstacle that comes your way. Whatever the wilderness throws at you, don't worry, have faith, hunker down, and get prepared, because you most definitely have what it takes to hack it! Thank you for reading this book!

FREE Bonus Reminder

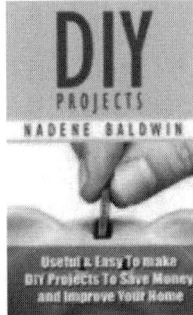

If you have not grabbed it yet, please go ahead and download your special bonus report *"DIY Projects. 13 Useful & Easy To Make DIY Projects To Save Money & Improve Your Home!"*

Simply Click the Button Below

OR **Go to This Page**

http://diyhomecraft.com/free

BONUS #2: More Free & Discounted Books or Products

Do you want to receive more Free/Discounted Books or Products?

We have a mailing list where we send out our new Books or Products when they go free or with a discount on Amazon. Click on the link below to sign up for Free & Discount Book & Product Promotions.

=> **Sign Up for Free & Discount Book & Product Promotions** <=

OR Go to this URL

http://zbit.ly/1WBb1Ek

Printed in Great Britain
by Amazon